Whenever
Your Attitude Stinks...
Read This

or

Will be President for Food

by Wayne Allred

Illustrated by
David Mecham

♦ A WILLOW TREE BOOK ♦

Published by:
WILLOW TREE BOOKS
Box 516
Kamas, Utah
84036

ISBN 1-885027-08-7

Cover Design & Layout by David Mecham
Printed in the United States of America

willow @ allwest.net
www.willowtreebooks.com

Since you are reading this book, you probably are not swimming for your life while being pursued by hungry sharks or trapped inside a whale at the bottom of the sea.

IV

Why worry?

Either you are well, or you are sick.

If you are well, you have nothing to worry about...except global warming, the new strains of super penicillin-resistant bacteria, gang violence, and how you're going to pay for your kids' education.

If you are sick, you have only 2 things to worry about: Either you will get well so you can keep worrying about the fat content in your hoagie sandwich, the tenderness in your glands which could be cancer, or large asteroids which could collide with the earth in this century...or you will die.,

If you die, you have only 2 things to worry about (in addition to whether your husband will finally hook up with that old girl friend from college after you're dead, who you think he likes better than you anyway, what your friends really thought of you, depletion of the Ozone layer, and the build up of chemical weapons in the third world) either you will go to heaven, in which case you have nothing to worry about...except for whether or not your neighbor, Max, is there, who you hate...or if it's really going to be as boring as it looks...or you will go to hell...which can't possibly be worse than all of this worrying...or...which will be a relief because everyone knows that the things you conjure up in your mind are never as bad as you think they will be...and you can finally quit worrying about going there and just enjoy it...

W.A.

Contents

Introduction

Since I wrote this book, many people have asked me questions like: "So what makes you think you could be leader of the free world and butt of two thirds of the jokes in America?" Like me, I'm sure that most of you probably think this is a pretty stupid question. While I'm not too swift intellectually, maybe I'm not a complete imbecile. Of course, like most of my readers, I frankly have no more interest in having the responsibility of being president of the United States than the rest of the human refuse that seriously ran for the office last election. Even a starving bum like me would have to be nuts to want that job. The truth is, like most actual presidential candidates, I was only interested in the food, ...and of course, the other perks.

Imagine if you can, hundreds of gorgeous babes throwing themselves at you. Imagine being driven everywhere in your own private limousine. Imagine hanging out with all the celebrities in the world. Imagine being able to spend 4 years of your life without any concern whatever for being honest, moral, responsible, or for telling the truth...that you could do anything you wanted, anything you could conjure up, regardless how dishonest or degrading, with complete impunity because you are "The President of the United States."

And not only do you enjoy absolute

immunity from prosecution, but you also have an unlimited budget, most of the money in the free world, to spend on public relations...you could pay the best actors and public relations people in the world any amount to stand up and not answer questions about your character and behavior. So, in answer to the question, "Why do I think I could be president?" The obvious answer is, "I could do that."

If you think about it, even the actual job can't be all that tough. It looks to me like all you have to do is wet your finger, put it into the political air and then go with the flow. If everyone wants a better job, put them to work for the government. If they want more pay, give them a triple hefty raise... and then double that. If they are tired of working and would rather have most days off... give it to them. Call it your "personal R&R leave Bill."

Of course, the one problem that can arise is when a challenger comes along and has the gaul to offer them more of everything than you did. Therefore, you must anticipate this and do two things: 1. Expect what people are going to want and give it to them before they can ask for it, and 2. Be ready at a moments notice with a smear campaign to personally destroy the reputation and credibility of anyone who opposes you.

Some, who aren't too thoughtful, worry about those responsible people out there in voter land who wonder how we're going to pay for all of these jobs and handouts. Don't give them a second thought. There will never be enough boring, responsible, narrow-minded, industrious, working people to be able to out-vote the rest of the country. Plus, if as president, you're careful to destroy the special interests of all of the people who didn't vote for you, they'll soon get the message.

You may ask, "What if someone exposes the fact that I just want to be president so I can be mean to people I hate and to get loose women?"

Lie. Even if they have you on a camera holding up a bank, now days, if your lawyer goes on TV and denies everything, insisting that you were home baking cookies for the bigoted policeman who beat you up, this is enough to create reasonable doubt. Besides, if you get kicked out of the presidency, you can always be a senator or congressperson. There are lots of them. While they don't get paid quite as much and are real unpopular, they still get lots of free stuff and plenty of loose women.

But I should clarify...this is not a political book. I didn't come here to talk politics. I'm just an observer of human nature who thinks I should probably throw my hat into the presidential ring and who writes to avoid having to do any real work.

The real purpose of this book is to explore the concept of happiness, to hone in on the collective psyches of John Q. Public, to update you on the state of modern mental health...at least the stuff that's entertaining, and to give you an excuse for all of that whining that you're just going to do anyway.

We know our readers and how easily they can become confused. This book is about feeling good no matter what kind of reprobate you are, no matter how bad you screw up your and everyone else's lives around you. Even if you're a shiftless, lazy loser, no matter; you can still feel tolerably good. We'll explain how. So stop thinking like a responsible adult for a minute, shift your brain into auto pilot and read on.

Editor's note: After publishing our last book, "The Outhouse Book," there were some loser-whiners who called or wrote to complain because we insulted them and then failed to insult someone else to their satisfaction. While we do our best to insult everyone, with the ever growing number of special interests, ethnic and religious groups, and whiney, pouty, sorry losers, it is becoming increasingly difficult to properly insult everyone. So, if we have overlooked your particular tender spot or special interest, we sincerely apologize. Please understand; it's not because we didn't want to insult you. We will try our best to offend as many people as we can while using, in our judgment "good taste." What more can we do?

Thank you

I How to fix a screwed up life

It seems like Sir Winston Churchill, Don Knotts, or somebody once said, "For every person digging at the root of a problem there are 100 hacking at the leaves."

I, frankly, can't see the point. Problems have absolutely nothing to do with vegetables, unless, of course, politicians get hold of them, then there's green stuff hanging all over everything along with plenty of fertilizer which usually just serves to make the problems grow bigger. No, rather than going to work on the greenery, I plan to start by solving the actual problems themselves...starting with the problem of your misery, unhappiness, despair, neurosis, psychosis, schizophrenia, or mad cow disease.

Fact: Most unhappiness is caused by people doing stupid things. So let's go to work and solve the problems of the stupid things that YOU do. I will do this by first outlining some of your problems and then offering solutions which might work. The following are a few examples of this problem solving technique:

Problem #1: Hitting the wall with your head.
Solution #1: This is stupid. Stop doing this.

Problem #2: Stupidity.
Solution #2: This is a very big problem. If you are stupid and annoy people, they will generally do mean things to you, which could make you unhappy. Buy the book, "How to Cope When You Are Surrounded By Idiots...Or If You Are One", By Scholar, Social Scientist, and world-renowned author, Wayne Allred, wherein are the answers to your problem of stupidity. If you do this, it will also help me solve...

Problem #3: Poverty, not having enough money.
Solution #3: The problem of money is normally one of perspective; Either you don't have as much as the people around you or the people around you have too much when compared with you. You must decide which and take the appropriate action. For example, if you don't have enough money relative to those around you, you can solve this problem if

you move to a place where people are poorer. If you live in Beverly Hills and feel poor, if you were to move to say, Rock Springs, Wyoming, you might just fit in perfectly after you picked up some boots and Wranglers. If, on the other hand you already live in Rock Springs and you feel poor compared to those around you, you might have to move someplace really radical like Pakistan or Bangladesh. This change of perspective should make you feel terrific.

Problem #4: Stapling your lips to your forehead.
Solution #4: This is stupid. Stop doing it.

Problem #5: Ugliness and Unpopularity.
Solution #5: Being ugly and unpopular can really put a damper on life. Some people, like your mom, will tell you "Just be yourself," and stuff like that. However, if you are ugly and unpopular, "yourself" is the last thing you should be since nobody already likes you and everyone treats you like dirt. No, you need a complete make-over to forcefully compel people to like you.

　　　Change everything. If you have long hair, cut it short. If you are skinny, become fat. If you are quiet and shy, start being a pushy loudmouth. If you don't smoke or drink, start.

　　　Try this for a while, and if you still don't have enough friends, you might have to resort to the tried and true method of buying some. (If you

3

don't have enough money to buy friends in the place where you live, you may have to down-grade your place of residence as described above.)

<u>Problem #6</u>: Stubbing your toe on the bed post in the night while you're going to the bathroom.
<u>Solution #6</u>: Use duct tape to fasten stuffed animals or chickens to all of the low hard stuff where you might stub your toe in the middle of the night.

<u>Problem #7</u>: You are a total screw up.
<u>Solution #6</u>: Read the next chapter. ◆◆

2 When you are a screw-up

When it comes to working with the screw ups of life, now days it is very important to assess blame. If this mess you call your life is somebody else's fault, you need to know about it so your lawyers can determine the amount of damages to claim.

Herein often lies the problem: Many bumbling incompetents are bumbling around in complete ignorance of their own incompetence. If they had any idea what colossal screw ups they were, some of them would stop.

In view of this, here is our contribution to science and therapy, some clues which should help you determine if you are a screw up.

You are probably a screw-up if:

When you were little, whenever people would come to visit your family, your parents would hide you in the trunk of the car or in the refrigerator.

You find yourself late for work for the third time this week because you had to rummage around to find something to put over your head after you inadvertently grabbed the blow torch instead of the hair dryer again.

You lost your license to practice body piercing because your first 200 customers all died from loss of blood.

While you are sure that you don't have an eating disorder, you keep getting thrown out of restaurants because you're so enthusiastic about your new weight loss program that you can't wait until you get to the bathroom to put your finger down your throat...so you throw up all over the salad bar.

For the fourth time this month, you inadvertently placed the bank bag full of money into the trash receptacle at Bacon Queen Restaurant and deposited your left over chicken nuggets in the over night bank teller.

You are a career politician.

Before you lost your license to practice thoracic surgery, on many occasions, after sewing up the patient's body cavity, his hospital 'jammies stuck out a long ways in front and you realized that it was the antenna from your TV or some other appliance from the hospital break room which you inadvertently left inside...and you repeatedly spot-welded your patients' butt-cheeks together.

At work, your associates will let you near only one computer: a 1979 IBM Pteranadon II with 2.5 bytes of RAM and 5 bytes of memory on a 5 inch floppy, because it seems that every time the whole company computer network goes down dumping everything in the system, you happen to be the one standing next to the guilty computer terminal with a stupid look on your face. And, defying all known laws of physics, you alone have proven capable of erasing all company back up files...sometimes even from a neighboring state.

Because of hundreds of little accidents over the years, you now are left with only one finger on each hand; the middle one. Your family thinks this might be a sign from heaven.

This week your boss, the chef, has made you start keeping track of what happens to the plates you drop. You are proud because you discovered that of the 33 plates you dropped this past week, 11 went directly onto the floor, 5 you caught with your foot and while the food spilled, at least you were able to keep the plates from breaking. Only 18 went into the laps of your customers.

The last time you bought a $1.79 part which you were going to personally install to fix your toilet, 2 days later you wound up calling a plumber at $50.00 an hour, a carpenter and an electrician at $60.00 an hour each and a ground crew from N.A.S.A. to unscramble the mess and get your neighbors televisions and dishwashers working again before they start a class action law suit.

After 4 years as a fishing tour guide, you celebrated having your first customer catch an actual fish...even though it weighed only 2 ounces and even though it flung itself into the boat while going after a mosquito.

It's now November. You left on your first cross-country trip driving a truck for a national company last July and today, after spending these four months driving around from state to state hopelessly lost and in 2nd gear (the only one you can find) today you finally delivered that load of tomatoes to the wrong grocery store.

Although you passed your written law enforcement tests with flying colors, you suspect that you are nonetheless in trouble because you have just finished accidentally shooting your fifth person this week for a parking violation.

After all of your bad experiences, you now refuse to accept a blind date without having your lawyer listen in on the conversation and then having your prospective date sign a 200 page pre-datual agreement.

While you don't consider yourself an alcoholic or drug addict, your family is leaving you because you are drunk or loaded most mornings by 8:00 a.m. even though you no longer have to get up that early to go to work because you can't hold a job.

No one has seen your hod carrier for 2 days. And all that you can figure is that you must have bricked him into that wall you just finished.

As a veterinarian, you get regular calls complaining that the cats you were supposed to have neutered are still capable of reproduction, but they have to drink their milk through a straw, and have voices that sound like Louis Armstrong.

These are the kinds of clues that you look for to determine if you are a screw up. However, for some of you, we need to be a little less subtle, (subtleties confuse you) so we have come up with this test. So, if you're still not sure whether or not you are a screw up, try this:

1. Your car breaks down 120 miles from nowhere. Do you:

A. Use paper clips, bubble gum, and sunflower seed shells from the floor of your car to improvise a by-pass of the carburetor and solve the problem, getting you quickly on your way again.

B. Lock your doors and wait for a highway patrolman to drive by and ignore you.

C. Lie in the road screaming in agony because you forgot to take the car out of gear and, as you were getting out, it rolled over your feet crunching all of your metacarpal bones as it accelerated off a 1000 foot cliff nearby.

2. You sit down to take a test which will determine your future income possibilities. You:

A. Take a deep breath and relax looking forward to this opportunity to "show off" what you know because of your diligent hard work.

B. Carefully get your cheat sheet out of your false arm cast and position yourself where you can get a good look at your neighbors' answer sheet so you can check your answers.

C. After a brief chat with some of the other applicants, you get out a coin to flip and a flask of emergency whiskey from your purse because you realize you devoted 6 months of your life to the study of the wrong material.

3. Your septic tank has backed up. Do you:

A. Do nothing because you don't have a septic tank.

B. Put on your hip waders, rubber gloves, gas mask, get your tools and fix it.

C. You wade in with every tool you own only to emerge 3 weeks later naked, with your hair burned off, and acid burns over 90% of your body and all of your tools and olfactory facilities irretrievably lost in the mess which, thanks to your efforts will have to be completely replaced.

If you answered "C" to any of these, unless you are on some kind of heavy medication, you are most likely a screw up. ◆◆

3 Success through lower expectations

"It's better to aim your spear at a star and hit the ground than to throw a pipe bomb at a cat and hit your uncle Melvin's Winnebago."

-Enid Thoreau

Imagine having more money than you can spend. Picture yourself on your own yacht cruising the Caribbean with beautiful people all around you, waiters catering to your every whim. Imagine being able to travel anywhere you want, to buy huge houses, castles with cash. Imagine being able to afford a new Dodge 4X4 pickup.

Now, by contrast, picture yourself dodging

those bill collectors in your '78 Datsun complete with 214,000 actual miles and those trendy rust spots. Imagine working a job you detest, with people who hate you, dining on beans and franks...Hey, if you don't have to imagine this because this is your life, lighten up. Don't get all huffy! Didn't I promise you success? Read on.

"What does imagining these two contrasting lifestyles have to do with your success", you ask? Frankly, not much, but it helps to get you into a fantasy frame of mind if I'm going to get you to comprehend this next concept: "How to become a success in life."

"The secret of success."

One day while flipping channels, I inadvertantly put my thumb on the volume button instead of the channel changer which caused the volume to go up instead of changing channels. Before I could get off from the channel I was stuck on, my neighbors and I heard a very loud motivational speaker give the following dictionary definition of success:

Success: "The achievement of a goal."

Light bulbs went off all over the place in my head. Then and there my life was changed forever. I suddenly realized the truth that if a person expects to throw up after eating caviar, whenever she does throw up from eating caviar, she is a success. When a person expects to fall on his face while ice skating...and then does...he is a resounding success.

Never before or since has one idea affected me so profoundly. From that day forward I became a huge success and you can to if you can only understand and apply this concept in your life:

"You can be successful in life only if your goals and expectations are below your actual achievements."

What this means is that if you are currently a miserable failure, all you have to do to become one of the world's great success stories is to work to get your expectations lower than your actual life. If you are able to achieve those lowered goals and expectations, by the dictionary definition, you are a success. Isn't that amazing?!? Don't you love it? You can do this!

For an example, let's say you and your spouse live in a tumbled down trailer (rented) and take in $1200.00 a month between you. If your goal has been to move into your own home in a nice suburban neighborhood, on that income you're just setting yourself up for failure and dis-appointment. If, instead, your goal was to move into a garbage can and earn $30.00 a month redeeming the bottles you pick up along road sides, right now you would have to be considered one of the great success stories in the world.

Some of you out there might have some reservations using this tactic. Stop it right now! Hey, don't feel guilty. After all, the U.S. government has approved this method. They do it all the time. When not enough applicants can qualify for elite military and fire fighting groups, they simply lower the standards, thereby raising the self-esteem of all of those people who would have had to go find jobs for which they are more suited. When too many kids who haven't applied themselves in high school can't pass the exams to get into college, they simply dumb down the exams. With so many kids failing school right now, there is a big movement afoot to eliminate grading standards altogether! If we can just get those expectations low enough, some day every child in America will be a resounding success.

One of the ultimate examples of this concept which you are all familiar with is how we've lowered standards for the president of the United States to the point that even if you have made a few mistakes, like...say...you smoked pot, or you dodged the draft, or, while, of course you are a philanderer, you messed up and weren't terribly discreet a couple of times, and you cheated on your taxes, or maybe you are a pathological liar without any shame at all or without so much as one shred of common decency. Hey, No problem. Now days even you can still be elected! Go for it!

Now, with an understanding of this important concept, go be the biggest success in the world. Make your realities your dreams. ◆◆

4

Reasons why you should be happy even though your life is a complete disaster

So you're down. We need to cheer you up. No matter what your circumstances, if a 900 pound squid has removed your mask and snorkel and is clinging to your face, if your two year old daughter has hold of your nose hairs and is flipping you around, even if the company you work for has just announced that they are laying you off and on the way out of his office, the boss gave you a noogie with a cheese grater...and then squirted you with analgesic...you can still keep a stiff upper lip, a chipper attitude even without strong medication. Consider:

❑ Your lips and ears haven't been stretched behind your head and spot-welded together.

❏ You probably didn't realize just at this moment as you are falling through the air that you forgot to connect the bunji chord to your leg.

❏ Your insides aren't on the outside of you.

❏ Even though you are so ugly you can't coax a dog to come close enough for you to pet it with a steak in your hand, your ugliness frees you to do things that attractive people can only dream of...like wearing a full-body tattoo, trying new kinds of acne medicine you found in the high school shop, and pressing your face against the window to scare people at fancy restaurants.

❏ Cat owners don't control congress.

❏ It's still legal in this country to buy a balloon, inhale the helium, and talk like a Munchkin.

❏ You're not a mackerel attached to a pop gear trolling for marlin.

❏ Since you are reading this book, you probably are not swimming for your life while being pursued by hungry sharks or trapped inside a whale at the bottom of the sea.

❏ You are not a turnip.

❏ Although you are so poor they just repossessed your wheelbarrow and starving kids and condemned your cardboard shack so they can try to eradicate the vermin in town, you have a very low tax rate.

❏ Even if your daughter was blonde, she probably didn't date O.J.

❏ Although you belong to a family of drug-crazed, violent, part alien, cross-dressing, hermaphroditic lunatics, there is no law that requires you to go on Oprah and humiliate yourself by bearing your soul.

❏ Your head hasn't fallen off.

❏ Although you totaled your car, it was no big deal because it was only worth $600.00. Other people you know have cars worth $900.00 or even $1,000.00. In fact, the guy who you ran into must be much more unhappy than you because his car was worth upwards of $1,200.00!

❏ You don't melt when snotty little kids throw water on you.

❏ There is currently no law forcing you to eat caviar, anchovies, sushi, oysters, rocks, or gravel.

❏ Your intestinal parasites don't have conversations with you.

❏ You chuckle to yourself because although your wife has kicked you out because you're a bum and your lawyer says that you will now have to pay her two thirds of your crummy $1600.00 per month salary for alimony and child support, what she doesn't know is that you have just been diagnosed terminal from a rare disease. She will only be able to collect 2 or 3 months worth before you croak.

❏ Your nose is running, but at least it's not dripping battery acid.

❏ Although you've been audited by the IRS and so now they're taking your house, boat, car, groceries and spleen and levying your pay check for the next 170 years, you had a $1.25 profit from the sale of your Upper Deck John Crotty rookie card and since there is no way they can trace the transaction, you're not going to tell them...plus your house has fleas in the rug...and your spleen has a tumor.

❏ You probably don't live inside a zit.

❏ Even if you lack the fundamental intelligence necessary to wallow successfully in a wet corral, you can still vote, watch network TV, have children and work for the government.

❏ A cow is not sitting on your head.

❏ You are not yet calcified or petrified.

❏ Even though you're broken hearted because, after 9 years you finally gave up waiting and broke up with your boyfriend because he's unable to make a commitment. It works out for the best because later on you realize how lucky you are because you read in a tabloid that he's really a cross-dressing woman with a deep voice who is a bigamist and who makes her living fleecing other women...and all he/she got from you was your Hundai Excell.

❏ Your face isn't being used as a sledge.

❏ Most dentists don't use chain saws.

❏ Even though your politicians have nothing but contempt for you and are convinced that you are a mush-headed sap who can be manipulated at their every whim by well produced media ads, and because they can threaten to use their influence to do you harm, they will most likely never have you hunted down and killed because they like having your tax dollars to spend whenever they want.

❏ Your colon isn't connected directly to your nose.

❏ Your ears probably don't drag on the ground.

❏ Bacteria don't grow to be as big as cows.

❏ Alien worm-like creatures aren't dangling from your nostrils. ◆◆

5 How to speak to an idiot

One of life's most frustrating experiences is dealing with idiots - confirmed and unconfirmed. Some time ago I wrote a column and subsequent book chapter about politically correct terms to use when describing an idiot. Judging by the response I got from some of my scarier readers, this must have been one of my most useful columns ever. Because we are forced to deal constantly with idiots, knowing how to productively interface with them is one of life's most useful skills. Besides, if we are to have any success at all improving your self esteem, we've got to confront this perplexing problem at some point. For those of you who have trouble communicating with idiots, I have compiled this list of additional terms to use.

When speaking directly to an idiot:

(Some of these phrases were actually yelled at me by people who I cut off in traffic...so you know they will work.)

❏ It's time to pull over and change the air in your head.

❏ You've obviously been affected by standing under a pile driver for all of those years.

❏ Your kid may be an honors student but you're still an idiot.

❏ You know, you seem to me to be the kind of person who might be more comfortable in a fish tank.

❏ Pardon my driving, I'm reloading.

❏ It wouldn't be fair to have a battle of wits with an unarmed man.

When discussing an idiot with other people:

❏ He was actually pretty smart once until they dropped that tractor on his head.

❏ That's what happens when they allow two Democrats to marry.

❏ Her original brain was hit by lightning.

❏ His family was too poor to buy glue so he grew up sniffing feet.

❏ I hear he once lost a chess match to a Jell-O mold.

❏ He really does remarkably well considering his father was a geranium.

❏ Some people are only alive because murder is illegal.

❏ The institution she escaped from specializes in keeping brain-dead patients alive.

❏ He was born with his cranium filled with nasal hair.

❏ Mildew scored higher on the ACT test.

❏ His older bothers must have held his head in the toilet a little too long.

When waxing philosophic:

❏ That just goes to show that if there's enough chemicals in the drinking water, the evolutionary process can be reversed.

❏ She's proof that even with an IQ of only 2, you can still pass kidney stones and annoy other people.

❏ When he was little, his mom poked beans up his nose.

❏ Make things idiot proof and someone will design a better idiot.

❏ This is the result of a mother eating too many boxes of pencil lead during pregnancy.

❏ She just hasn't been the same since she accidentally swallowed that table saw.

When you're angry:

(Remember, releasing your anger by using demeaning and sarcastic terms when addressing imbeciles is better than blowing up an office building or shooting dozens of innocent people.)

❏ Go ahead. Honk your brains out; it won't take long.

❏ Hey, somebody lit your brain stem on fire!

❏ Forget world peace. Visualize your turn signal.

❏ Ever stop to think and then forget to start again? ◆◆

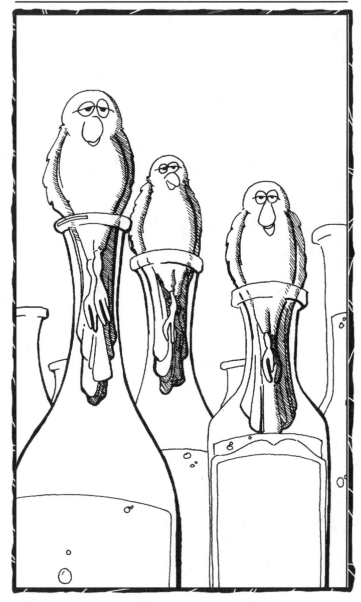

6

Failing with humans? Maybe animals will make you happy

If you're a total failure with people, some experts in the psychotic professions suggest that you get a pet for companionship instead of setting yourself up for more failure by continuing to insist on dealing with human beings. If this is the direction that you decide to go, there are some things you should know about those pets...cats especially. Very soon, on the outside of all cats, the government will require one of the following warnings to be posted:

WARNING: A tom cat will eat his own children if given a chance.

WARNING: The main cause of the plagues of the

1300s, which wiped out over half of the population of medieval Europe, was the proliferation of black rats who were host to the fleas which carried the disease. This explosion of rats was made possible when people who believed that cats were possessed by demons did everything in their power to wipe them out. An absence of their main predatory opposition allowed the rats' population to explode. So, from the logic of Washington DC., because cats are possessed, they were responsible for the plagues of the middle ages.

Additional useful information about your pets which you should consider before using them for therapy:

❏ Because of their unique ability to mate with themselves or to grow into two complete animals when chopped in half, about the only way that I have found to successfully spay or neuter an earthworm is to drop it into a blender.

❏ Buck Hyde of Bearskid, Montana once caught a 3 pound brook trout using only the nose ring of an adolescent (which he had accidentally hooked during his back swing while casting his rod) for bait. Even more remarkable is the fact that he did it with only the half of his fishing pole that was left after it was broken over his head and with most of the line wrapped around his neck.

❏ Gladys Pipp of Knights End, Wisconsin fed her pet Boa, George, a steady diet of fluoridated baby birds for 15 years. After he died, Gladys discovered that he still had all of his original teeth, as far as she could tell.

❏ We're wondering: if you put one of those fish with the transparent skin...You know the kind you can see right into...If you put one of those in an X-ray machine, would it make it so you COULDN'T see it's bones?

❏ Bats, when dipped in batter and deep fried, still taste pretty bad.

❏ A pet store's special promotion offering a free manicure for your pet lizard with purchase of over $500 was not a big financial success.

❏ While few pets would choke to death on a spaghetti noodle, many would die from swallowing a common household cheese grater.

❏ Another way to get your neighbor's pet guppies to swim upside down is to feed them lots of Jell-O.

❏ Danny Kidd, age 6, once played with a common 4 inch night crawler from the bait box until it is estimated by his uncle Ralph, that just before it snapped, it had reached a length of over 3 feet.

❏ Most common house cats will eat their weight in mice each week, provided that mice are available and that the cat is not too well fed. On the other hand, it will take nearly a month for one mouse to eat the equivalent of one cat...and you will probably have to put it in a blender.

❏ Not only do they sing continually, keeping unwanted friends and relatives away, but parakeets make wonderful bottle corks.

❏ Vietnamese, pot-bellied pigs often get so fat that their bellies will drag on the ground. If you lead yours over one of those tire-ripper things that they have at stadium parking lots, be sure you are going the right direction.

❏ Because their life span is so short, (roughly 2 days), fruit flies rarely suffer from the degenerative diseases that so plague mankind.

❏ Determined to pre-shrink the wool of the garments he produced like the cotton ones of his competitors, Henry Grizwold of Suffolk, New Hampshire boiled his 75 sheep until they became sheep soup. And the clothes still shrunk.

❑ While, for the first 300 years of our country's existence, and even today in some cultures, dog meat has been a favorite delicacy...I'm not aware of anyone who ever got hungry enough to eat a cat. ◆◆

When I am a cratchety, senile old bat, I will wear my underwear on the outside of my clothes

One of the main impediments to bliss and happiness is old age. After your bones get brittle and your muscles turn to mush and your sight disappears, you are pretty much left to getting your jollies by annoying younger people.

In fact, if you're an old codger, you're pretty much wasting your time reading the rest of this book, expecting me to tell you how to be happy and successful, rich, good looking and so forth. Forget all that at this point in your life and instead, change your perspective. Try to be happy doing something you have a realistic chance of succeeding at; namely learning how to be content with observing how bizarre behavior affects younger people.

If this is a new idea to you, you might try some of the following:

❏ Leave 5 or 6 crustified blobs of food in your whiskers or on your clothes.

❏ Go everywhere with your fly open.

❏ Wear hot pants to church...or if you're a guy, a Speedo.

❏ Practice blowing your nose as loud as you can in restaurants and other public places.

❏ Put your false teeth in backwards.

❏ Drive down the white line in the road blocking both lanes of traffic going roughly half the speed limit with your blinker on in your "57 pink Cadillac.

❏ Take a full 45 minutes writing your check in the express lane at the supermarket.

❏ Place a huge amplifier and six foot high speakers on the lawn and place a microphone on your pillow at night so the entire state can enjoy your snoring.

❑ Spray Round Up® on your neighbors' lawn and pets whenever they get within 6 feet of your property line.

❑ Park your car sideways taking the 3 stalls right next to the open handicapped spaces while displaying your handicapped parking decal. ◆◆

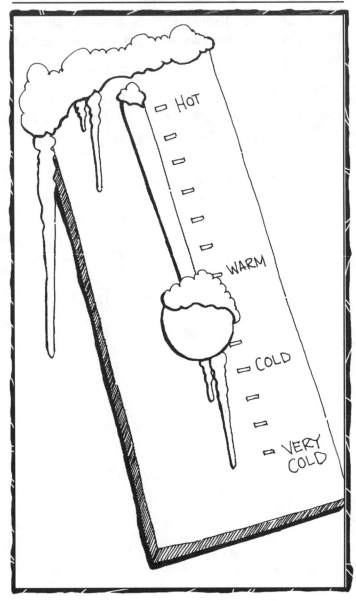

8 Funny stuff to cheer you up when you life is a screwed up mess

❏ Mel Brooks observed: "Tragedy is when I cut my finger. Comedy is when you fall into an open sewer and die."

❏ The reason why worry kills more people than work is because more people worry than work.

❏ Bumper Sticker: "IRS: We've got what it takes to take what you've got."

❏ Sympathy is what you give a relative when you don't want to lend him money.

❏ Sitting in a quiet, little restaurant in Wyoming, eavesdropping on a conversation at a neighboring table, I heard the best bit of common sense political wisdom I've ever heard in my life. (You have to figure that pure brilliance like this would have to come from Wyoming.) The woman there suggested to the people at her table that nearly all of the nations problems could be solved by doing only one simple thing: **Allowing every citizen in the US to shoot one person in their lifetime without fear of retribution or penalty**.

Think about this for just a minute. Can you imagine how much kinder clerks would be if they had to wonder whether or not you had used your shot. And visa versa too; would you be rude to a clerk or waitress if you knew that they might still have their one magic bullet? How fair would tax collectors, bill collectors, and neighbors be if everyone had to wonder if this last bit of rude behavior might be their last. How courteously would you drive in traffic?

Since that time, I have taken every opportunity to promote this idea, who's time (in my opinion) has come. I guess my main fear is that one of the main political parties will get hold of it and use it as part of their platform. And then if it is ever passed into law, the final version of the bill will be so convoluted that no one will recognize it.

❏ Cold! If the thermometer had been an inch longer we'd all have frozen to death!
- Mark Twain.

❏ The most beautiful flower in the world will kill you if you snork the petals up your nose.

44

❏ Dizzy Dean, explaining how he felt after being hit on the head by a ball in the 1934 world series: "The doctors x-rayed my head and found nothing."

❏ Bumper Sticker: "Laugh alone and the world thinks you're an idiot."

❏ The Canadian government consists of a prime minister, whose primary function is to meet with the U.S. president once a year and ask in a whiny voice how come we keep dropping acid rain on them. The president always replies that we'll stop the acid rain if they'll stop the cold air masses.
- Dave Berry.

❏ Politicians are like roaches. The problem isn't that they eat so much, it's just that they contaminate everything they touch.
- Bert Doshier

❏ Yogi Berra: "Always go to other people's funerals, otherwise they won't come to yours."

❏ Friends come and go but enemies accumulate.

❏ The proper office of a friend is to side with you when you are wrong. Nearly anybody will side with you when you are in the right.
- Mark Twain ◆◆

9 Relieve yourself of your peeves

Since we ran an article some time ago asking for readers to send in their pet peeves, we have been overwhelmed. Now everybody in the world must be whining to us.

Reading all of this whiney mail is really beginning to depress me and to get on my nerves. I guess it must be therapeutic to get stuff that's bothering you off your chest and so, since misery loves company, I figured, "Why not discharge my moral obligation and print a completely random sampling of these pet peeves so others can enjoy them too?" (Note: We have used their real names when legible. If you know any of these whiners, feel free to call them up and tell them to quit sending me their whining.) To that end, I offer:

More of my reader's pet peeves:

Misty Knight from Denver, Colorado, says that she gets angry every time someone yanks on the chain connected to the ring in her eyebrow, nose, or lip.

Bud Ligero from Phoenix, Arizona, hates it when a check made out to "Guido," that was intended to pay for illicit drugs, bounces.

Twila Spleen from Reesty Mulch, Oregon, hates it when coming out of a public rest room, her mini skirt gets tucked into her underwear in the back...especially when no one has the guts to tell her for two days.

Rex L. Ives from Bear Digit, Montana, gets upset every time he's making a big speech in public and his teeth fall out.

Ima Sapp, from Portland, Oregon, hates having all four wheels of his car jacked up, and then, after he's crawled underneath to change the oil, having one of his kids come and kick the supports out from under it.

Ashlee Hutchens, my daughter's friend

from just outside Hooper, Utah, thinks it stinks when she gets in @#*>! trouble for @#*>! cussing even though her @#*>! teachers cuss at her first.

Elleno Decaca from Animal City, Wisconsin, gets peeved whenever she's really car sick and someone opens a can of dog food right under her nose.

Rusty Clave from Septic Falls, Idaho, hates it whenever he asks a girl to dance and she runs screaming to call the police.

Madge from Bear Skid, Wyoming, gets really worked up whenever her husband, Scooter, gets the remote during football season.

Wesley Schmurtz from Amoebae Springs, South Dakota, hates it when aliens abduct people and then eat them just to satisfy their curiosity about how humans taste.

Sal Peter, from Philadelphia, Pennsylvania, gets upset whenever he and his buddies do a drive by shooting and then when they go by one more time every-body throws him out of the car.

Bart Hemlock from Farmington, New

Mexico, gets torqued at being dragged face down in the dirt behind his Jeep and having his nose fill up with rocks.

Patty Delfeo from Virginia City, New Mexico, hates it when her date puts a bag over her head and then forgets to take it off when he drops her off back at home.

Stu Carne hated it when he was feeding the last of the fish food from the urn on the window sill to his guppies and realized too late that those flakes were, in fact, the last remains of his Aunt Mildred.

Thorette Sharpe from Permawedge, Colorado, gets really upset when her new medication kicks in and she suddenly realizes that the person she was saying vicious things about is also the person she has been saying them to.

Felix Del Gato of Medicine Ditch, Washington, says he hates it whenever he's robbing a 7-11 store and his ski mask twists so that he can't see out the eye holes and so he walks into the closed doors as he's trying to escape.

Melvin Delgordo from Puckerbrush, Nevada, hates bunji jumping off a 1000 foot high bridge and realizing on the way down that he only connected the chord to the elastic on his Jockey shorts.

Dan Carafea of Verminberg, Arkansas, gets disgusted every time he has a hot date with a girl who loves cats, and then finds he has nothing to clean the fur and cat parts out of his grill, except for dental floss.

Ann Nesia from Roach Clip, Colorado, hates it when she falls asleep in class and her drool fills up her shoes.

Sandy Bottoms of Dumpling, South Dakota, gets really worked up when she wipes out while water-skiing with jogging weights on her feet and the boat forgets to come back and pick her up. ◆◆

10

More funny stuff to cheer you up when you life is a screwed up mess

❏ It's impossible to make anything fool proof because fools are so ingenious.

❏ New Jersey Nets guard, Leon Wood, to TV commentator, Steve Albert: "Are you any relation to your brother, Marv?"

❏ Bumper Sticker: "Whenever you do a good deed, get a receipt in case heaven is like the IRS."

❏ If you insist on hanging around the urinals, don't be too upset if you wind up getting soaked.

❏ There is no easy way to find out what the actual true price of any given car is. Oh, sure, there is a "sticker price," but only a very naive, fungal creature just arrived from a distant galaxy would dream of paying this. In fact, federal law now requires that the following statement appear directly under the sticker price:

"WARNING TO STUPID PEOPLE:
DO NOT PAY THIS AMOUNT."

-Dave Berry

❏ Women like silent men. They think they're listening.

❏ Shaquille O'Neal, on whether he had visited the Parthenon during his trip to Greece: "I can't really remember the names of the clubs that we went to."

❏ Bumper Sticker: "Reality is a crutch for people who can't handle drugs."

❏ Farmers' Union: The E.I.E.I.O.

❏ He is useless on top of the ground; he ought to be under it, inspiring the cabbages.

-Mark Twain.

❏ An old geezer and an old tire have much in common; they're bald in most spots with a bulge here and there; but if you patch the holes and pump them both full of air, one of them makes a pretty good flotation device.

❑ Bumper Sticker: Curiosity didn't kill your cat. My car did. ◆◆

II

Depression for all seasons

Throughout all of history, there have been people who would mope around and not do any work and just watch daytime soaps, and yell at their kids and scratch their scabs till they bled. We just thought they were living their version of the American dream or Mesopotamian dream...or else they were just nuts. And now, after all these years thanks to new scientific break-throughs, we find out that, in fact, these are symptoms of another disease needing billions of dollars to be studied. All along, we find that the root of these and thousands of other problems has been the disease now labeled "depression".

Furthermore, some say that this depression is not even a mental disorder. It is often caused by physical factors: chemical imbalance, the thorax being wrapped unnaturally around the hydrologist, an endocrine gland run amok causing it to secrete too much cyanide, testosterone, or adrenaline...or most often, a distortion of bank account balances between the medical community, the insurance companies, and the tax-payers who have a surplus of assets causing a fiscal imbalance.

Since, after hearing all of the problems depression causes and figuring that, judging by some of my mail, most of my readers must suffer from some form of depression, I thought it might be a good public service to pass along this information.

First of all, you probably aren't aware that most of you who suffer from depression have not yet been diagnosed. So that from now on you'll know, the symptoms are:

1. Being depressed.
2. Not having enough money.
3. Insomnia.
4. Your doctor doesn't have enough money.
5. Your dog has died.
6. Your girl friend has left you for another man.
7. You have left your girlfriend for another woman.
8. You have a desire to strangle people.
9. Sweaty palms.

10. Chronic fatigue.
11. Hair loss.
12. Depression.
13. Indigestion.
14. Shingles.
15. Depression.
16. Splotches.
17. Cratchetiness.
18. You hate everyone.
19. Depression.
20. Indigo.
18. Vertigo.
19. A feeling of helplessness, hopelessness, or ugliness.
20. Things sometimes go wrong in your life.
21. You are ornery or depressed.

Any of these symptoms along with most other ones that you or anyone else can think up could be an indication that you have depression.

How to be sure:

If you want to be certain once and for all that what you are suffering from is indeed clinical depression, take out your insurance policy and read the part under psychological disorders and how much they pay. If the figure is big enough to cover treatment, you definitely have a debilitating form of depression and you should get treatment immediately. If the diagnosis is wrong, just remember: It's not your money.

If you should, through a thorough reading of your insurance policy, discover that you don't have depression, at least not the kind covered in your insurance policy, we recommend the following home remedy: In a large bucket, mix up gravel, baking soda, jalapeno peppers and 4 random pills from those old bottles in the medicine cabinet that you have no idea whatsoever what they are...or were. Wash all of this down with a quart of vodka...or you can substitute a bottle of diet pills. This remedy, or a similar one that you come up with, should give you an attack of something covered even in your lame insurance policy...and short of that, at least an excuse for your bizarre behavior.

Another common type of depression that has been recently brought to light is sometimes called " masculine depression" and it is caused by men. The symptoms include the feeling that you don't have everything you want, that many men don't understand the way you feel, or the desire to have the material possessions that some man has without necessarily having to go to the trouble or risk of marrying him or of earning it yourself...or of voting Democratic.

If you suffer from this type of depression, we suggest the following relaxation treatment: Find a firm, but comfortable spot, preferably one that has wooden ties spaced about 14 inches apart connecting long steel rails. Lie down on the ties with your head resting on one of the steel rails and wait for the train to come. Or, you could take up the violin. ◆◆

12

An anger management technique from the aanals of history

In a smoky card room in an isolated backwater town in Colorado toward the end of the 19th century, old Jake is finally winning at poker...apparently too much. The steely eyed stranger, after losing his fifth straight hand, accuses him of cheating. The cards fly. Patrons dive for cover as both men back cautiously onto the dance floor. Feeling a sudden rush of adrenaline-induced courage, Jake calls the stranger a scrawny, bug-eyed, gap toothed, rattler-polecat with poor personal hygiene.

Jake draws, but not fast enough. Before he can complete the motion, he is hit in the face by a blast which knocks him backward into a puddle of beer spilled there by one of the now cowering bar patrons.

That quickly, in a split second, it's over. Clint, Jake, and Stanley stare in disbelief at the little plastic cowboy. This is their first loss in over 30 pretend, little plastic cowboy and Indian water melon seed gunfights.

Once again, although tempers flared, although insults were hurled back and forth, and even though the stranger is indeed a bug-eyed, gap toothed, rattler-polecat with poor personal hygiene, the locals are forced to admit that he can squirt a watermelon seed quicker and straighter than the best they can put forward. Thankfully, because these men were trained in the latest anger management technique, "displaced diversion" the story has a happy ending. They all shake hands and go back to playing BINGO.

This amazing anger management strategy was developed near the end of the civil War by Dr. Enos Freud as a part of a government funded program to reduce the number of war and card playing fatalities, to help those with a genetic predisposition to cowardice, and to provide jobs for the dozens of government workers who might otherwise lose their draft deferment. According to 19th century government records, many theoretical lives of family men who still enjoyed a good brawl, but who didn't want to leave helpless widows and orphans behind were saved by this innovative program.

This pioneering effort spawned dozens of

scientific social experiments, some of them quite entertaining and most expensive. Even today, progressive social scientists with big government grants and excessive time on their hands are devising programs similar to this in order to make the world a better place and insure that the amount of their department's entitlement to government funds doesn't get reduced. For example, programs have been devised to attempt to rehabilitate the youthful criminal element and give them a release for their anger other than by shooting someone or biting off a chunk of their ear. There have been programs such as midnight basketball, graffiti art, lighting cats on fire, and drive-by paint gun shootings (The weapons being similar to large cake decorators).

Some opponents to these programs ask, "Shouldn't we change strategies and make parents more responsible to raise their own kids?" and, "Where the government has to step in, maybe they could insist that the kids learn to work, and be responsible...and provide more parental, "when I was a boy or girl" lectures."

Opponents to these opponents, on the other hand, point out that many people don't want their kids to know what they were doing when they were kids, and that there isn't enough time in a modern day to expect parents to lecture kids like they used to. This is a job for school principals, and scientists receiving grants from government programs.

We think the government should give us a large grant to study "displaced diversion." ◆◆

13 Even more funny stuff to cheer you up when your life is a screwed up mess

❑ Bumper Sticker: "I didn't fight my way to the top of the food chain to be a vegetarian."

❑ A synonym is a word you use when you can't spell the other one.

❑ A turkey that knows how to bark has a decent chance of surviving Thanksgiving.

❑ One time Mark Twain arrived in town just before he was scheduled to lecture. Finding no reception committee, he walked straight to the lecture hall, where the crowd was gathering. As he tried to press through, he was stopped cold by the ticket-taker.

Said Twain: "It's all right, I am the lecturer."

The ticket-taker shook his head. "No you don't" he chuckled. "Three of you have got in so far, but the next lecturer that goes in tonight pays."

Mark Twain paid.

- From "The Wit and Wisdom of Mark Twain."

❏ Winston Bennett, former University of Kentucky basketball forward: "I've never had major knee surgery on any other part of my body."

❏ Bumper Sticker: "Women who seek equality with men lack ambition."

❏ I am particularly outraged by the charge that guys never help out around the house. I happen to be a guy, and often, when my wife goes away, I assume total responsibility for the household, and my wife has such confidence in me that she will often wait for an entire half-hour before she calls.

- Dave Berry.

❏ Former President Gerald Ford: "I watch a lot of baseball on the radio."

❏ Confidence is the feeling you had before you knew better.

❏ Old fishermen never die; they just get tangled up in their flies.

❏ Politicians are to virtue what a squid is to a helicopter.

❏ Bumper Sticker: But officer...The pedestrian had no idea which way to go, so I ran over him. ◆◆

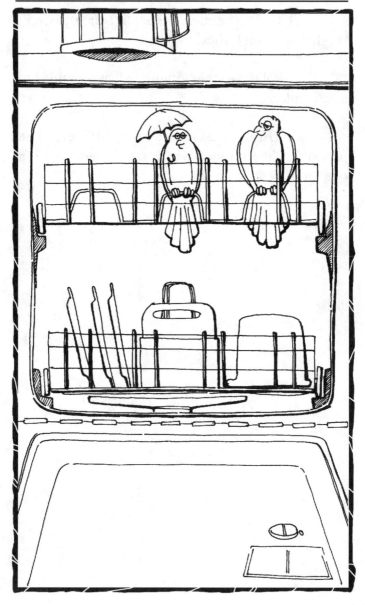

 Ask Dr. Angst

The following are excerpts from the mental health column written by Dr. Henry Angst which appears daily on his web site -www.Lobotomy.com

In addition to his pseudo professional duties, Dr. Angst, "Psychiatrist to the Internet", is also a veterinary gynecologist, a hang-glider tester, and works part-time as an automobile lubrication technician at "Greasy Lube."

Q: Last week my pet dachshund, Fritz, went berserk, crawled through the accordion exhaust tube connecting my dryer to the outside of the house and was subsequently run over while crossing the highway, trying to get to the neighbors' schnauzer who was in heat. His little carcass has been lying there for a week between the two white stripes getting flatter and flatter and looking less and less like a dachshund. Because he's been my only family, this has been a very traumatic experience for me. I have fallen into a depression that I can't get out of. Is there any way to replace this loyal canine love that I've lost?

--Edselene Quagmire, Slippery Pit, West Virginia

A: Dear Ms Mire, Many people find that the constant cheery chirping of a parakeet can help to bring them out of a depression and give them a new start. On the other hand, after 2 days with incessant parakeet chirping, my sister went off the deep end and ran hers through the "pots and pans" cycle on her dishwasher. So, try the parakeet and if it doesn't work for you either, try taking up a physical sport like rodeo, demolition derby or kick boxing.

Q: Years ago I experimented regularly with illicit recreational drugs. Later, both of my children were born normal, except, of course, for the gills and fins. However, I find that I am troubled by an occasional flashback. These seem to be increasing in frequency and intensity and picture brightly colored worms and grubs dancing the Macarena in annoying political info-mercials. Some happen at very inopportune times, like when I'm driving my Volkswagen microbus on the freeway. What do you suggest?   --Phil Armonic, Hog Smooch, S.D.

A: While there's probably nothing you can do to stop the flashbacks, since your brain is fried already, you could at least make enough money from selling those kids to the circus or aquarium to support a new drug habit. You might as well start again, since you drive a V.W. microbus and everyone, including the cops, will hassle you because they just assume you're a warmed-over, drug-crazed hippie throwback from the '60's.

Q: My boyfriend is leaving me for another woman who is better looking. In an effort to manipulate him and make him feel sorry for me, I have attempted suicide once by cutting my wrists with a plastic spoon and a second time by overdosing on my mother's MIDOL®. This strategy doesn't seem to be working. He doesn't act anywhere near as miserable and distraught as I think he should. What would a registered pseudo professional like you recommend?   --Melissa Del Gordo, Littleton, CO.

A: Melissa, next time try washing your pills down with battery acid or a good liquid drain cleaner.

Q: I am a compulsive liar. I am always getting caught but never seem to get into trouble. The real catch is that I absolutely love to lie. I lie for practical reasons, sport, and just for fun...about everything. (And I also like to wear women's clothing, go shop lifting with my wife, and beat the illegal aliens who clean my house, just for the heck of it.)

I wouldn't worry about my lying, but since I became President of the United States back in 1992, all of my close friends have gone to prison while lying for me and now they're starting to make me feel guilty too, because I won't do anything to get them out. This massive accumulating pile of guilt is starting to make me feel so low that I'm afraid I might commit suicide or something.

--Bill Smith (Not his real name) Washington DC.

A: Dear Mr. Smith: Okay.

Q: I am a very very very overweight, pudgy person who rarely thinks about my weight, which is excessive and embarrassing, because my clothes don't fit any more because I'm so fat. In order to get this extra excessive weight off, I do an hour of aerobic exercise 12 times a day. I also haven't eaten anything but water since August 30,1987 when I had a delicious, scrumptious glazed donut with lemon filling that was to die for. But I quickly put my finger down my throat so I don't think that any of the calories made it into my actual blood stream.

How can I get this extra weight off and still keep my healthy outlook on food and my body?

-- Bea Cormorant, Fort Vegemite, Nebraska

A: My Aunt Mildred had a weight problem like yours for a few years before she died. The thing that finally got every bit of unwanted weight off her was when she started a regimen of regular Mr. Clean, walnut shell, and Spun-glass enemas. (Don't try this yourself without doctor's supervision.) Unfortunately, just when she was about to finally reach her optimum weight, she died. We buried her inside a curtain rod. ◆◆

15

Odds & Ends

My Grandma Allred always said...actually, the type of things my grandma Allred always said were: "Merrill!" (That was my grand pa) "Get the mud off your boots before you step in the house!" and "Wayne!" (That was me.) "You can't be full. A growing boy like you can surely eat one more piece of pumpkin pie." (Grandma thought the reason why I was so skinny was because my mom, her daughter in law, wasn't feeding me and the only cure was a month at her house where she would sit on my chest and dump food into my mouth)...But, now that was a long time ago, and it had little to do with your crummy attitude. Besides, I think at some time, grandma might have said something like "Whenever you get tired of viewing the lead-dog's backside, you can always close your eyes and visualize a cheese burger." And she certainly would have wanted you to have a good attitude...and to clean the mud off your feet.

So to that end, the attitude stuff, not the dirty feet, I have compiled these bits of wisdom and information to help you through life and to help you develop a better attitude.

❏ A way to tenderize wild game, making it almost as tender as the backside of a cyclist who just finished a cross country trip, is to put it on the sidewalk or a flat rock, then beat it vigorously with a maul or sledge for an hour... Then pick up the fibers remaining, being careful not to get cement or rock chips in the mix. Marinate these over night in Liquid Plumber. Even if it tastes kind of lousy, you'll find that whatever's left will be the most tender meat you ever ate.

❏ Season your stew with anything you want, but don't let your buddy, Stu, go into the forest during hunting season in his Rudolph costume.

❏ When your basement's already filled up with water, it's probably time to turn the guppies loose and let them have some fun.

❏ Many vegetarians, long plagued by nutritional and immune system deficiencies are finally getting some relief using a good old fashioned treatment. Researchers at Gump State institute for Sociopathic Medicine have found that they get fewer colds and have more energy when they pick up a little extra protein from the common cereal weevil usually found in their granola and Grape Nuts. Dr. Aanos Brainmold insists that since he started a daily regimen of not picking out the weevil in his Granola...combined, of course, with an hour-a-day of aerobic exercise, consistently getting his 8 + hours of uninterrupted sleep since his kids moved out, sneaking an occasional Big Mac on the side, added to his weekly gelatin, bean sprout and tofu enemas, and since they finished his chemotherapy, his energy level has tripled...and he hardly gets sick any more.

'Atta boy Doc!

❏ To cure memory loss...

If you suffer from memory loss, don't spend the big bucks for Alzheimer's treatment, electric shock, or a brain transplant, simply roll up a newspaper* and hand it to your spouse. Have him or her whack you over the head when you forget your kids' names.

If your spouse is the one with the failing memory, just reverse the process.

Let's say you told your husband that you

wanted a new diamond tennis bracelet for your anniversary. A week later, you bring it up again and he doesn't even remember the conversation. Grab the rolled-up newspaper, repeat your request for the diamonds and whack him a good one. Repeat the process until memory improves.**

If newspaper is in short supply, you can also use an umbrella, hockey stick, shovel or rake, etc...

** *One caution: If the instrument is too heavy or too sharp (I.E. a sledge or maul) instead of enhancing memory, it could sometimes actually serve to impair it slightly. This can be bad. Use caution.*

❏ Unless you like phlegm in your scrambled eggs, it's best to wait to complain about the food until after the meal is eaten.

❏ If you feed stray dogs, maybe you can convince them to poop on your neighbor's lawn out of respect...or then again, maybe instead, they will have babies in your garage.

❏ People who sneeze too much should avoid poking grass up their noses.

❏ The best way to make a baby stop crying long enough to take a picture is to hand them a lemon slice.

❏ As a bonus, you get entertaining pictures.

❏ Whenever you're fixing breakfast for the Pope, let him put his own tabasco on his eggs...and be sure that the biscuits and gravy haven't been in the fridge more than a couple of weeks.

❏ Unfortunately skunks rarely die with their backsides buried in the ground.

❏ If you're truly concerned with what other people think about you, then don't wear your underwear on the outside of your clothes.

❏ For an interesting and authentic Halloween costume which also clears up pimples for a day or two, try washing your face with broken glass. (Note to slower readers: This is a joke.) ◆◆

Glossary: gloss/eh/rhee - A collection of textural glosses.

Glossary of mental
health terms

Bulimia:

That annoying thing some girls do whenever they see someone they think is really disgusting and they do a kind of sign language thing where they put their finger part-way down their throat and fake like they're going to throw up...and then laugh.

Compulsive behavior:

Stuff that's real fun but which you don't want to do too often...like putting your tongue on a battery or staying up all night to watch the Star Wars trilogy and eating pizza.

Euphoria:

The feeling of bliss and extreme happiness that actors apparently feel whenever they are being filmed in a commercial.

Ivan Pavlov

(Also known as "Ivan the Terrible"): The twisted, neurotic foreigner who spent billions of government dollars in bogus research projects. When finally they threatened to cut off his grants, he wrote this lame paper about how his drooling dogs could trick him into ringing a bell or something. Amazingly, they bought off on it and now he's famous, but also pretty much dead as far as we know.

Mad Cow Disease:

A dangerous condition where whenever afternoon TV ratings in the agricultural working section of the world dropped off, and so to teach people a lesson, Oprah, who had just squished another bathroom scale flat, declared herself a temporary vegetarian immediately influencing all the people in Western Civilization who don't want to get jobs because that would mean they would have to miss "The Show" to stop eating Big Macs which caused the beef prices to plummet which, in turn, made all the cows mad...and it didn't help the ranchers either.

Narcissism:

Similar to Exorcism, but because it's a bigger and harder word, fewer people understand it...while I understand it perfectly.

Neurosis:

A term that's useful in explaining other people's weird behavior. Whenever they really get on your nerves, you can call them neurotic. i.e.. When your son wants to play football, but your ex-wife won't sign the release, she could be called neurotic. Now that you mention it, all ex-wives are usually neurotic.

Psycho analysis:

The act of trying to understand what is going on between the ears of someone who is a neurotic, (see above) bone- headed, nitwit and then talk things through and make them comprehend what anyone else in the universe with an IQ over 2 can see is obviously going on, and to get them to do the sane, rational thing that you want them to before they screw up their lives. Very difficult to accomplish over the phone.

Shrink:

What happens to your bank account whenever you have to pay for treatment.

Sigmund Freud:

Chinese rock singer who's real name was "Pink Freud" who casted his rock videos using the "couch" method. He made jokes about guys who spend most of their time thinking about sex...and football. He was eventually accidentally destroyed when he tried to save Pavlov's dogs because they were being put to sleep because they were too old to drool any more. I think he signed the Declaration of Independence, or the Treaty of San Juan Guadeloupe or something too. Truly a pioneer mental case.

Xenophobia:

A silly word which proves that spelling in the English language was invented by schizoid nut cases or foreigners...or, they could have been playing some kind of practical joke in which case my respect for them just went sky high, otherwise...take for example "Xenophobia" which is spelled "xenophobia" when, if I or any other sane, rational, American-speaking adult were making up the spelling rules around here would be spelled "feer ov zenuh." And how about all these other words which make absolutely no sense like "rhythm" or "chamois" or "paradigm", which, without my daughter's help, I can't get close enough to the correct spelling for the spell-checker on my computer to correct. ◆◆

A touching letter from one of my readers.
*The following is an example of the kind of
fan mail I get daily:*

Dear Mr. Allred,

I am a 17 year old High School junior who feels compelled to write this letter to share with you how your books have changed my life.

Just a few short months ago I was in terrible shape. I was addicted to heroine, PCP, LSD, R.F.D., and B.F.D. I was Moll to the head gangster in the gang, the Weasel Turds, and I'm embarrassed to admit having cheated on him for the whole time with a Teflon® salesman who was named George until we got caught and they shot him. To give you an idea what a disaster my life had become, I even slumped so low that I sold my body to get money to buy illegal cough syrup and a pair of Doc. Martins. For a while I was an Iraqi spy. I had poor personal hygiene, refused to do my home work, was an assassin, ate red meat, voted for the Clintons and was a litter bug. Few non-politicians I know had ever sunk so low.

Then it happened. I found one of your books in the dumpster I was sleeping in. I read for hours, unable to put it down. The riveting humor, the caustic social analysis, the disgusting booger humor so inspired me that I determined then and there to turn my life around.

Now, I am happy to report that drugs,

except for regular doses of penicillin and a special shampoo for recurring head lice, are a thing of the past. You will be pleased to know that after reading your second book, I was so inspired that I started going back to school regularly and turning in my homework. I now have a 5.0 GPA and was recently elected homecoming queen and cheer leader. Just this week, I received word that I have been accepted into Harvard Medical School and I've been invited to be the first teenage astronaut.

I want you to know that if you're ever on drugs or find yourself donating to the DNC, should you ever want to get back into teaching, a position with the post office, or as President or something, please feel free to use my name as a reference.

Sincerely, you're devoted fan and groupie for life,

(Name withheld)

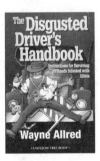

Willow Tree Book Order Form

Book Title	Quantity	x	Cost / Book	=	Total
			$5.95		
			$5.95		
			$5.95		
			$5.95		
			$5.95		
			$5.95		
			$5.95		
			$5.95		

Do not send Cash. Mail check or money order to:

Willow Tree Books   P.O. Box 516 Kamas, Utah   84036
Telephone 435-783-6679
Allow 3 weeks for delivery.

Quantity discounts available. Call us for more information.
9 a.m. - 5 p.m. MST

Sub Total =

Shipping = $2.00

Tax 8.5% =

Total Amount Enclosed =

Shipping Address

Name:

Street:

City: State:

Zip Code:

Telephone: